HABITAT SURVIVAL

OCEANS

Claire Llewellyn

Raintree

Chicago, Illinois

www.capstonepub.com
Visit our website to find out more information about Heinemann-Raintree books.

To order:
☎ Phone 800-747-4992
💻 Visit www.capstonepub.com to browse our catalog and order online.

© 2013 Raintree
an imprint of Capstone Global Library, LLC
Chicago, Illinois

Edited by Nancy Dickmann, Kristen Kowalkowski, and Claire Throp
Designed by Philippa Jenkins
Original illustrations © Capstone Global Library Ltd 2013
Illustrations by Oxford Designers and Illustrators, and Words and Publications
Picture research by Tracy Cummins
Originated by Capstone Global Library Ltd
Printed and bound in China by CTPS

16 15 14 13 12
10 9 8 7 6 5 4 3 2 1

Library of Congress Cataloging-in-Publication Data
Llewellyn, Claire.
  Oceans / Claire Llewellyn.
    p. cm.—(Habitat survival)
  Includes bibliographical references and index.
  ISBN 978-1-4109-4598-3 (hb)—ISBN 978-1-4109-4607-2 (pb) 1. Ocean—Juvenile literature. I. Title.
  GC21.5.L64 2013
    577.7—dc23   2012000237

Acknowledgments
We would like to thank the following for permission to reproduce photographs: Agefotostock p. 28 (© Tim Rock/WaterFrame); Biosphoto pp. 24 (Pierre Huguet), 26 (Gilles Martin); Dreamstime p. 22 (Eskasi); FLPA pp. 4 (Michael Weber/Imagebroker), 8 (Norbert Wu), 14 (Luciano Candisani), 15, 16 (Flip Nicklin/Minden Pictures), 18 (Mike Parry/Minden Pictures), 25 (Mark Newman); National Geographic Stock p. 29 (Gerry Ellis/Minden Pictures); Nature Picture Library pp. 7 (Jurgen Freund), 20 (David Fleetham); Shutterstock pp. 5 (© CyberEak), 11 (© Brett Atkins), 12 (© vilainecrevette), 17 (© Krzysztof Odziomek), 23 (© Vlad61), 27 (© Melvin Lee); Superstock p. 13 (© Pacific Stock).

Cover photograph of a butterfly fish reproduced with permission of Getty Images/Georgette Douwma.

Every effort has been made to contact copyright holders of any material reproduced in this book. Any omissions will be rectified in subsequent printings if notice is given to the publisher.

Disclaimer
All the Internet addresses (URLs) given in this book were valid at the time of going to press. However, due to the dynamic nature of the Internet, some addresses may have changed, or sites may have changed or ceased to exist since publication. While the author and publisher regret any inconvenience this may cause readers, no responsibility for any such changes can be accepted by either the author or the publisher.

Contents

Some words are shown in bold, **like this**. You can find out what they mean by looking in the glossary.

The World's Oceans

The world's oceans cover a huge part of our planet. They stretch from seas along the **coast** to vast, open waters. They sink down many miles to the seabed below. As well as deep and shallow water, the oceans contain rocky **coral reefs**, forests of seaweed, and the solid ocean floor. They form the largest **habitat** on Earth.

The seas around tropical coasts are shallow, warm, and clear. Further out, the water deepens and darkens.

The oceans are home to thousands of animals, from tiny corals and tropical fish to reptiles, such as turtles.

Ocean life

Thousands of plants and animals live in the ocean. Gigantic whales swim in the deep, shellfish crawl over rocks and the seabed, and many tiny living things float on the surface.

This book looks at how plants and animals have **adapted** to life in water and how they depend on one another to survive. It examines how humans affect the oceans and how our actions can threaten sea life or help it to survive.

How many animals?

Scientists have worked hard to count all the different types of animals in the sea. They know of nearly 250,000 kinds, but they believe that there could be more than one million.

A Watery Habitat

There are five great oceans on Earth, but they all flow into one another to make one huge body of water. Near the **equator**, the water is warm. Near the **poles**, the water is cold and the surface freezes over.

Ocean waters are shallow around most **coasts**. They are deeper further out, mainly about 2–4 miles (3–6 kilometers) deep. Seawater is very heavy and presses down on anything that's in it. This is called **water pressure**.

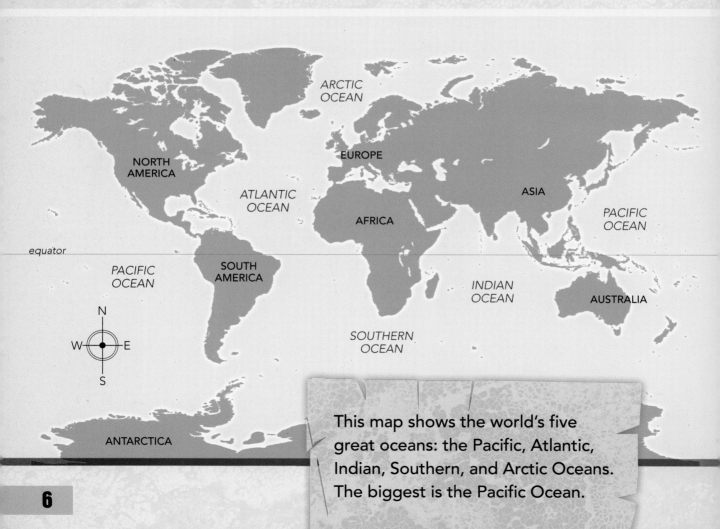

This map shows the world's five great oceans: the Pacific, Atlantic, Indian, Southern, and Arctic Oceans. The biggest is the Pacific Ocean.

Moving waters

The oceans are never still. Winds blow across the surface, making waves. Oceans also contain moving **currents**. They carry cold water toward the equator and warm water toward the poles.

Rivers carry water and **nutrients** to the sea. All living things need nutrients to grow. In the ocean, nutrients also come from dead animals and plants that **decay** on the seabed.

Warm current

In the Atlantic Ocean, there is a current called the Gulf Stream, which carries warm water north from the **tropics**. It flows past Ireland and the United Kingdom and makes winters milder there.

The Ocean Zones

Ocean waters are not all the same. As you go deeper, the water gets cooler, the pressure is greater, and there is less light and food. The different levels of the ocean are called zones, and each one has its own forms of life.

The fangtooth fish lives in the deepest parts of the sea. At night, it swims up to feed in shallower waters.

SUNLIGHT ZONE

Sunlight zone (0–660 feet/0–200 meters). The warm, bright sunlight zone is full of life. Near **coasts**, where the seabed is not deep, sea plants grow in the mud. Many different animals are found here. Further out, this zone is rich with tiny, floating animals and plants and the fish that feed on them.

The ocean zones form different kinds of **habitats**, which are home to different creatures.

TWILIGHT ZONE

Twilight zone (660–3,300 feet/200–1,000 meters). In the deeper twilight zone, the water is darker and colder. Animals such as sponges live on the seabed. In places where the seabed is deeper, whales and salmon swim through the gloomy water.

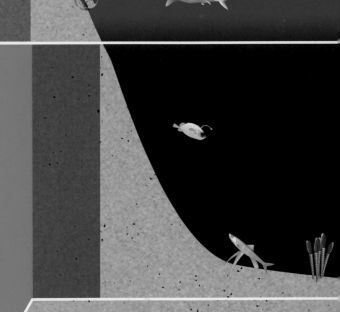

MIDNIGHT ZONE

Midnight zone (3,300–19,700 feet/1,000–6,000 meters). In the deepest part of the ocean, it is totally dark and cold, and there is crushing **water pressure**. Some deepwater fish, such as angler fish, make their own light to attract **prey**. Other animals feed on food that rains down from above.

Breathing in Water

Like all animals, sea creatures need to breathe **oxygen** in order to survive. Oxygen is found in the air, but it mixes well with water, so it is also found in the sea.

Breathing with gills

Fish take in oxygen from water using **gills** on the sides of their head. The gills are packed with tiny blood vessels. As a fish swims along, water enters its mouth and washes over its gills. The oxygen enters the blood and is then carried around its body.

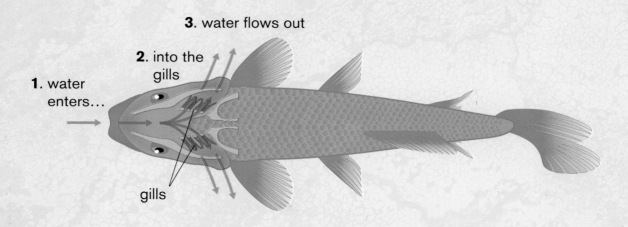

3. water flows out

2. into the gills

1. water enters…

gills

Fish use their gills to take in oxygen from the water. So do many other ocean creatures, such as sea slugs, mussels, and crabs.

Dolphins do not have gills. They must swim to the surface to breathe in air.

Breathing with lungs

Large sea **mammals**, such as dolphins, have lungs instead of gills. Reptiles, such as turtles, also have lungs. These animals have to swim to the surface to fill their lungs with air. They hold their breath while they dive. When the oxygen is all used up, they return to the surface for more.

Sea snakes

A sea snake's lungs run almost the length of its long body. The lungs are much larger than those of land snakes. They hold so much air that sea snakes can stay underwater for up to two hours.

Moving in Water

Sea animals move in different ways. Some types of jellyfish simply float in the water. They are carried along by the wind and **currents**. Other animals make their own way through the sea.

This jellyfish moves with the wind and currents, but it can use muscles inside its body to move up or down in the water.

Shooting along

Squid, octopuses, and some jellyfish move by sucking water inside their bodies and then squirting it out fast. The force makes them shoot backward— just like a balloon when the air inside it escapes.

Fish, **mammals**, and reptiles swim through the water. They have smooth bodies that slip easily through the sea. They also have powerful fins and flippers. They use these to move, steer, and stay upright in the water.

Seals are fast and graceful swimmers. They are heavy and clumsy on land.

Most animals need to stay at the surface, where there is lots of **oxygen** and food. To avoid sinking down, some fish trap air inside their bodies. Others store oil in their bodies, because it is lighter than water.

Staying put

Some sea animals do not move at all and may stay in one place all their lives. Corals fix themselves to rocks or the seabed and catch food as it passes by.

Plants in the Sea

Many plants are found in the sea. Plants need light to grow, so they are found in the sunlight zone near the surface of the water. The smallest sea plants are tiny **algae**. There are many different kinds and, together, they are called **phytoplankton**.

Sea grasses grow on sandy seabeds in places where there is warm, clear water. These plants have proper roots, which take in **nutrients** from the sandy floor. They are an important food for many animals.

Seaweed

Seaweeds have strong, rubbery stems that can ride the waves. Some have pockets of air called bladders. These keep their stems afloat so that light can reach them.
Seaweeds do not have proper roots. Instead they have a "foot" called a holdfast that holds on tightly to rocks.

A green turtle grazes on sea grass. Sea grasses are important **habitats** for many animals.

Forest in the sea

Kelp grows very fast. In summer, when there is plenty of light, it can grow 20 inches (50 centimeters) a day. Kelp grows in thick forests off colder shores. Some kelp forests are 70 feet (20 meters) deep.

Feeding at Sea

The oceans are full of food—from tiny plants to large, meaty fish. When you look at what eats what in the sea, the best place to start is with the **phytoplankton**. These tiny plants make their own food and do not eat anything else.

Phytoplankton are the smallest plants in the sea. They use sunlight to make food for themselves. They are then food for the **zooplankton**, the tiny creatures that float in the water. Most of them feed only on plants.

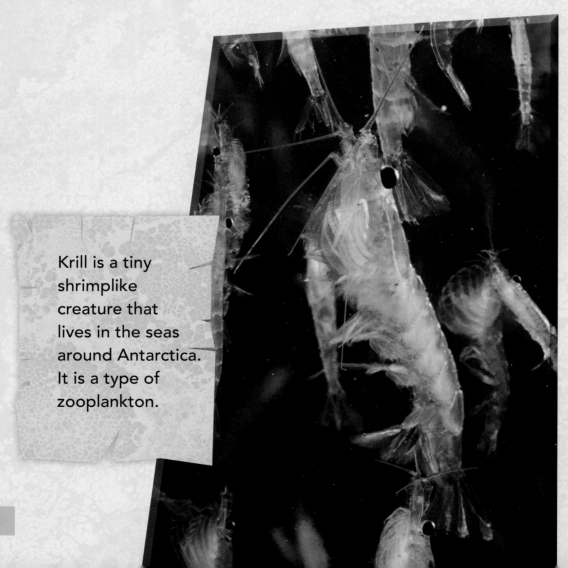

Krill is a tiny shrimplike creature that lives in the seas around Antarctica. It is a type of zooplankton.

The mighty whale shark feeds on plankton. It catches these tiny plants and animals by sucking water into its mouth and straining it out through its **gills**.

Zooplankton is very important in the ocean. Many animals feed on it—from small sardines to whale sharks, the largest fish in the sea.

Murky water

Cooler seas look murkier than tropical waters. This is because they contain more plankton. There are more storms to churn up **nutrients** from the deep, and this makes the sea a richer place for plants and animals to grow.

Hunting at Sea

Many sea creatures hunt one another. Some, such as sharks, hunt alone. They use their senses to find their **prey** and can sniff blood from a long way away. They are fast swimmers and have strong jaws and sharp teeth.

Hunting together

Some animals hunt in packs. Killer whales will work together to tip a seal off the ice and chase it through the water. They prevent the seal from swimming up for air, while taking turns to come up for air themselves. Soon the seal grows weak and is caught.

The great white shark has powerful jaws with up to 300 teeth.

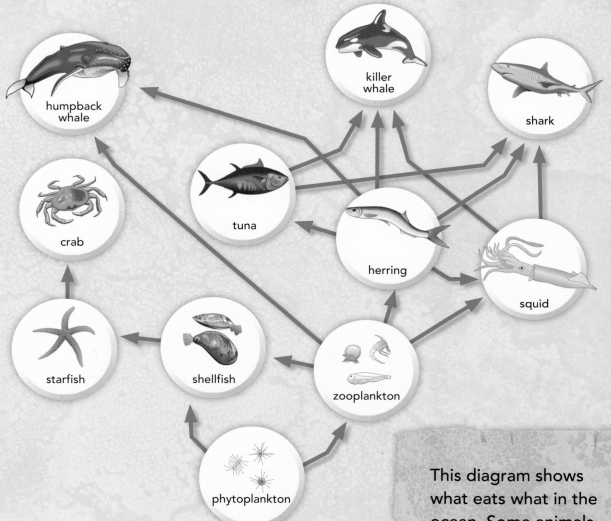

On the seabed

Many animals lurk on the seabed, catching food as it passes by. **Sea anemones** grab prey with their **tentacles**. Sponges suck water into their bodies and filter it for scraps of food. Garden eels live in burrows in sandy seabeds and feed on plankton carried in the **current**.

This diagram shows what eats what in the ocean. Some animals feed on plants. Larger animals feed on smaller animals.

On the Defense

Animals don't want to be eaten. They try to defend themselves in many different ways. Many animals hide on the seabed. The plaice has a flat body that blends in well with the sand. This makes the fish hard to see. Octopuses hide on rocks. They can change color to blend in even better.

A passing hunter will not spot this octopus that blends in so well with the corals on the reef.

Dark or light?

Like many fish, salmon are darker on top than they are below. If a hunter is swimming above them, it may not see their dark shape against the darkness of the sea. If the hunter is below them, it may not spot their silver belly against the lighter waters above.

Safety in numbers

In the open ocean, there is nowhere to hide, so many small fish live in big groups called shoals. The shoals are easy targets for hunters, but each fish has a better chance of surviving than if it swam on its own.

Flying fish

Flying fish swim in shoals. These fish have very long fins. At times of danger, they open them like wings, leave the water, and fly through the air. This helps them to escape from hunters.

A Coral Reef

Coral reefs are the most beautiful **habitat** in the ocean. They are found in shallow, tropical waters and are built by animals called coral polyps. The tiny polyps grow hard skeletons to protect their soft bodies. To do this, they depend on **algae**, which grow inside their bodies and provide them with food. Some corals catch and eat **zooplankton**, too. Over time, the polyps spread, and their skeletons form a reef.

Coral polyps are small animals that live very closely together. They have **tentacles** to catch food in the water. Many corals have hard skeletons that form coral reefs.

Corals come in many different colors and shapes. So do tropical fish.

Life on the reef

Coral reefs are full of color and life. They are home to bright tropical fish, sea horses, sea snails, sponges, and clams. Larger animals, such as turtles, sharks, and manta rays, visit the reef for food. Coral reefs are to the sea what rain forests are to the land: they are home to more kinds of animals and plants than any other ocean habitat.

Great Barrier Reef

The Great Barrier Reef in Australia is made up of over 3,000 different reefs. It is home to over 400 different kinds of coral, 500 kinds of seaweed, 1,500 kinds of fish, 16 kinds of sea snake, and 5 kinds of turtle.

Polluting the Sea

Sea life is very precious, but humans can harm it. One of the ways we do this is by **polluting** the water with litter and **poisonous** chemicals.

Litter

Many people treat beaches like a trash can. Plastic bottles and bags wash out to sea and can be deadly to sea life. Turtles mistake bags for jellyfish, one of their favorite foods. If they swallow the bags, the turtles can die. Other trash dangerous for sea life includes fishing line and nets, six-pack holders, kite string, glass bottles, and aluminum cans.

A sea turtle approaches a plastic bag, mistaking it for food. Plastic injures turtles and can cause them to suffocate, starve, or drown.

This starfish is coated in black, sticky oil. Oil spills threaten all sea life.

Poisonous chemicals

Industry and farming take place on land, but their chemicals can wash into rivers and flow into the sea. There, they poison small sea creatures. As larger animals feed on them, they get poisoned, too.

Oil pollution is very harmful. Thick, black oil leaks out of tankers or from oil wells on the seabed. Oil is light and floats to the surface, coating and poisoning animals in the sea.

Dangers to Sea Life

Fishing is threatening life in the oceans. People have always fished in the sea, but the human population is much bigger today than it was in the past. This means we are eating more fish, which can lead to **overfishing**. Every year, fishing boats take millions of tons of fish from the sea. As a result, fish numbers are falling.

This fishing boat in the Indian Ocean has caught a huge haul of tuna. Some kinds of tuna are overfished and are now **endangered**.

Some kinds of fishing are very harmful. Trawlers are fishing boats that drag heavy nets along the ocean floor and damage the seabed. Drift net fishing uses very long nets that hang in the water. Drift nets often trap dolphins, turtles, and sharks.

When coral polyps die, they turn white. This is called coral bleaching.

Global warming

Global warming is another danger. As our planet heats up, the oceans warm up, too. In **coral reefs**, warmer water kills the **algae** that the polyps depend on for food. As the polyps die, other sea life disappears, too.

Disappearing sea otters

Sea otters are disappearing from the Pacific **coast** of North America. Fewer fish in the sea has left seals and sea lions hungry. As seal numbers fall, the killer whales that once hunted them are hunting otters instead.

Saving Sea Life

Many people are working to protect the seas. Marine scientists study life in the ocean. They discover which kinds of fish are **endangered**. This helps governments to set limits on how many can be caught.

Good or bad tuna?

Dolphins often get killed in drift nets put out to catch tuna. Some countries have banned the sale of tuna unless it has been caught with fishing poles and lines.

This marine scientist makes a note of species living on a **coral reef**.

The Great Barrier Reef Marine Park lies off the northeastern **coast** of Australia. It is the largest marine reserve in the world.

Marine reserves

Many countries are setting up marine **reserves**. Marine reserves are like parks in the sea. No one is allowed to fish there, so fish numbers can grow. Some organizations want nearly half of all oceans protected in this way.

Make a difference

Some problems, such as **global warming**, need to be solved by governments. But we can all put our litter in the trash can and try to use fewer chemicals. We can buy fish that are plentiful and avoid ones that are not. Together, we can make a difference. Earth's oceans are precious, and we must protect them.

Glossary

adapt change in order to survive in a particular place

algae very simple plants that mainly live in water

coast where the land meets the sea

coral reef rocky ridge that grows up from the seafloor. It is made up of living coral and coral skeletons.

current moving band of water in the sea

decay to break down and rot away

endangered threatened with danger of dying out

equator imaginary line that circles Earth at its widest point

gill part of the body used by fish and other animals to breathe underwater

global warming slow and steady rise in Earth's temperature

habitat place where a plant or animal lives

mammal warm-blooded animal that usually has fur or hair and drinks milk from its mother when it is young

nutrient substance that is taken in by an animal or plant to help it grow

overfish reduce the number of fish by too much fishing

oxygen gas that is found in air. All living things need oxygen to survive.

phytoplankton tiny plants that live in the sea

poisonous dangerous substance that can cause death

pole point at the very top or bottom of Earth, where it is always cold

pollute spoil a place with litter or other harmful things

prey animal that is hunted and eaten by others

reserve area set aside for the protection of plants and animals

sea anemone brightly colored polyp with a cluster of tentacles

tentacle long, thin part of the body, often used for feeling

tropics parts of the world that lie close to the equator and are always warm

water pressure force of water as it pushes down

zooplankton tiny animals that float in the sea

Find Out More

Books

Callery, Sean. *Ocean* (Life Cycles). Edina, Minn.: Kingfisher, 2012.

Hynes, Margaret. *Oceans and Seas* (Navigators). Edina, Minn.: Kingfisher, 2012.

Savage, Steven. *Oceans and Seas* (Explorers). Edina, Minn.: Kingfisher, 2012.

Internet Sites

Facthound offers a safe, fun way to find Internet sites related to this book. All of the sites on Facthound have been researched by our staff.

Here's all you do:

Visit *www.facthound.com*

Type in this code: 9781410945983

Places to visit

Monterey Bay Aquarium
Monterey, CA
www.montereybayaquarium.org
See a kelp forest and large ocean fish at the Monterey Bay Aquarium, which works to inspire conservation of the oceans.

Shedd Aquarium
Chicago, IL
www.sheddaquarium.org
See some ocean animals, including dolphins and beluga whales, at the Shedd Aquarium.

Index